It's Time For Legato

Dear Sir/Madam,

"Legato" is, for the piano, one of the three possible types of articulation, that is, ways of producing sound from the instrument. In my opinion, it is the most challenging one. The reason behind creating this book was the scarcity of music publications dedicated to the subject of legato playing on the market. As a piano teacher myself, I spent a long time searching for a suitable book that would enable me to thoroughly introduce students to this topic. Most textbooks treat this issue too superficially, which I consider a mistake. Therefore, based on many years of my own experience and observations, I developed my own manual.

When playing legato, special attention should be paid to proper wrist movement. They should be relaxed, positioned appropriately high, and raised before starting each slur. If the wrists remain low and stiff, and the student solidifies these incorrect habits, further learning becomes uncertain. It is impossible to play with a beautiful, mature sound, have good keyboard control, and master the skill of phrasing when the hand and wrist muscles remain tense.

A significant number of students require many appropriate exercises to master the correct playing technique. This book serves as a guide to learning legato playing. It contains numerous well-structured exercises that will help the student understand and master the proper technique.

All exercises are written in the simplest "Middle C Position," which further facilitates learning. The student does not need to concentrate on reading unfamiliar notes, but can instead focus their attention on proper hand guidance.
I hope that this book will be a valuable and engaging tool for music teachers and contribute to better progress among students.

Joanna Bernat

The difference between portato and legato

1

portato

A

legato

portato

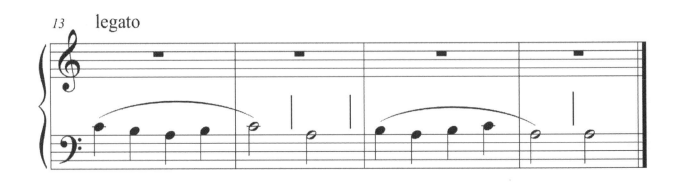

B

legato

2

portato

legato

portato

legato

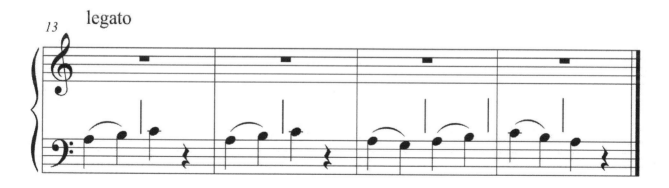

3

portato

A

legato

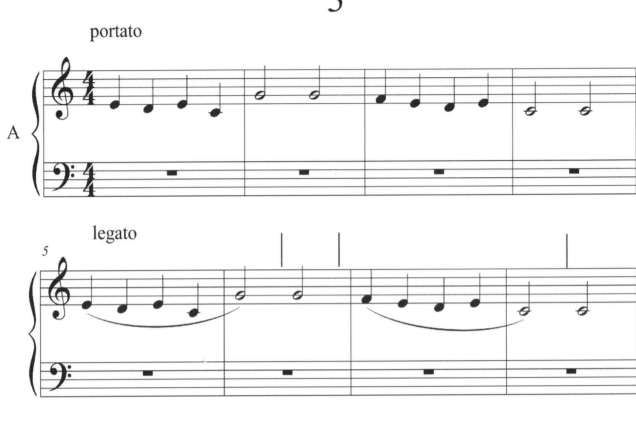

portato

B

legato

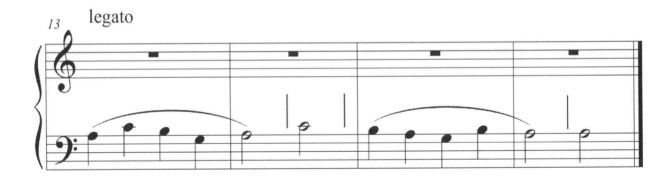

4

potrato

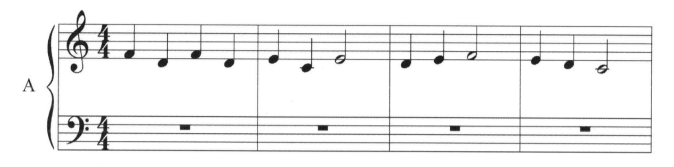

legato

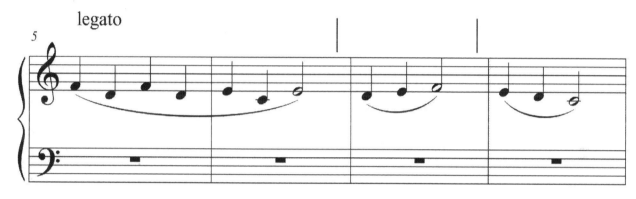

portato

legato

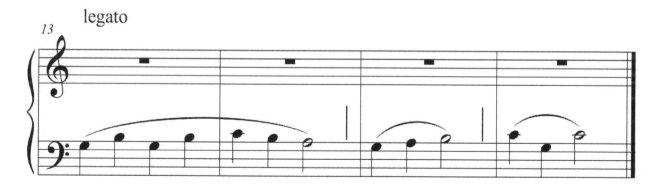

5

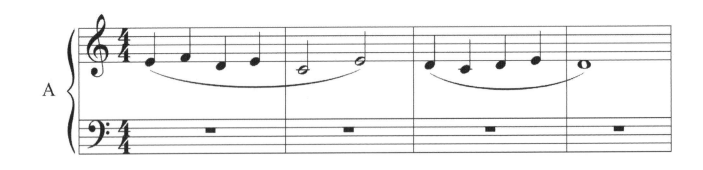

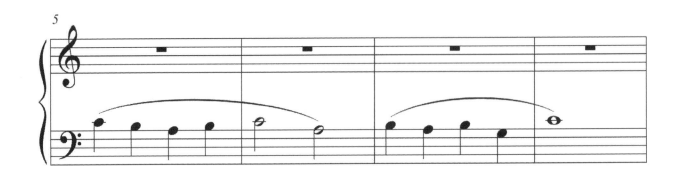

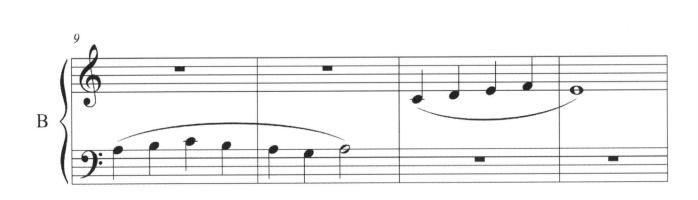

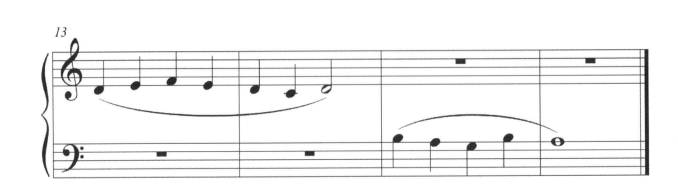

6

7

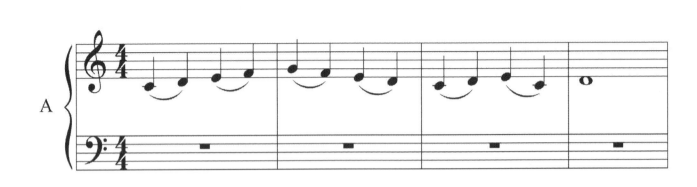

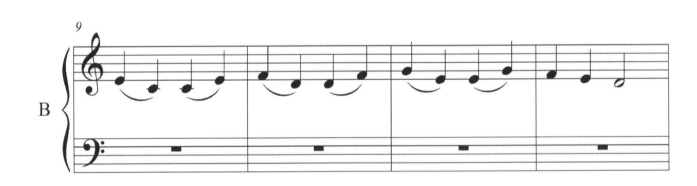

8

9

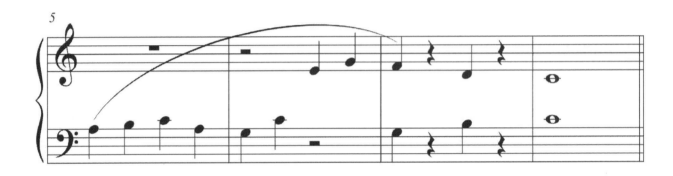

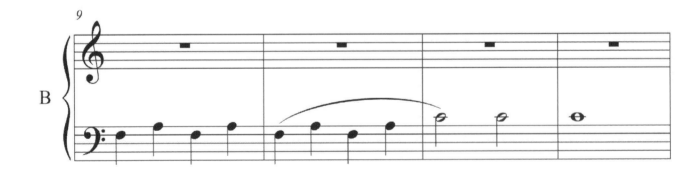

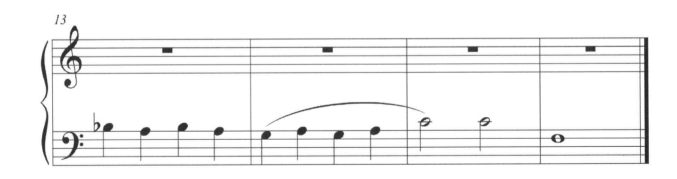

10

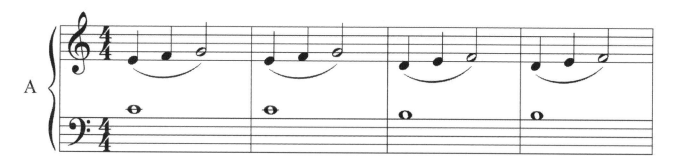

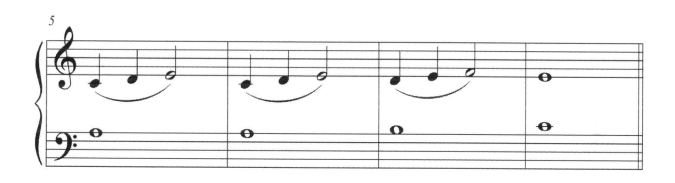

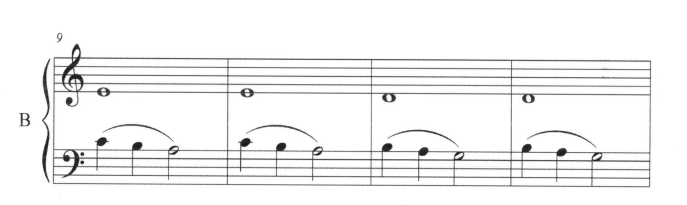

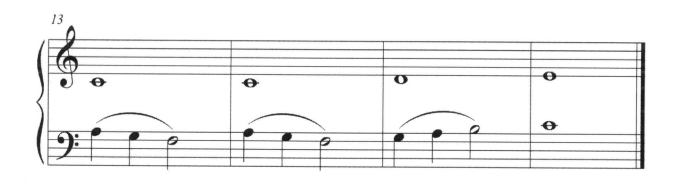

11

A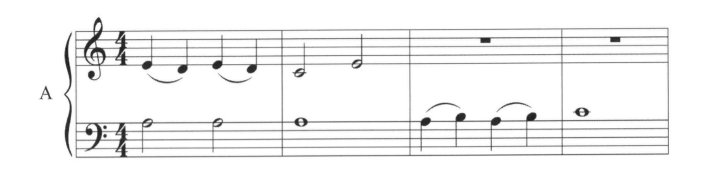

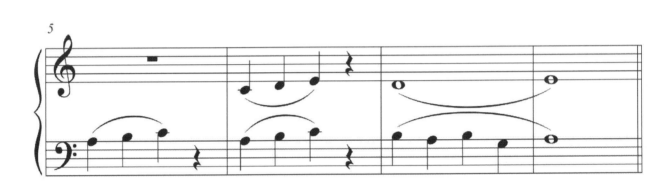

B

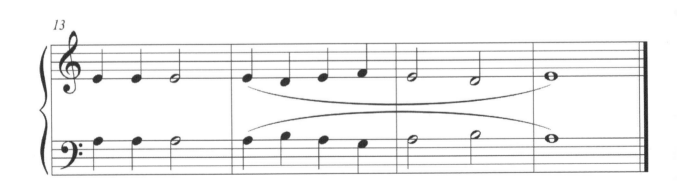

12

13

14

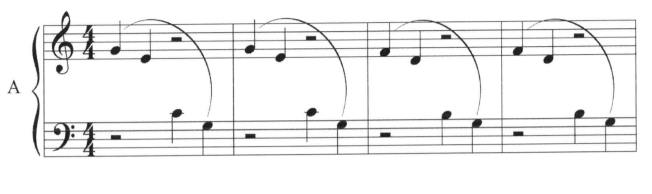

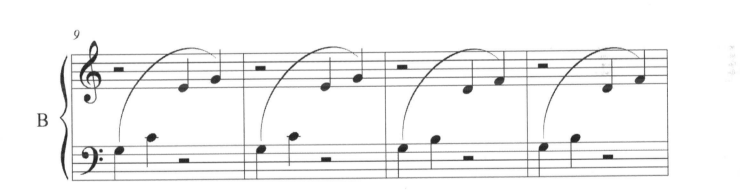

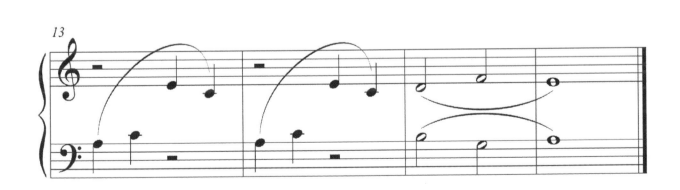

15. Sad Waltz

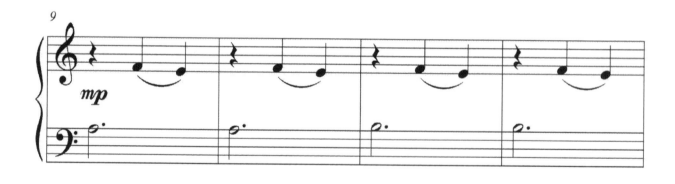

16. Happy Waltz

17. The Rainbow

18. The Old Castle

19. Talking to the Moon

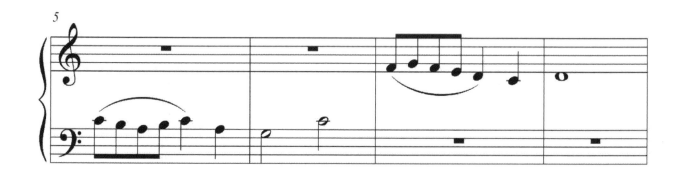

20. Happy March

21. Winter Wind

22. Evening Song

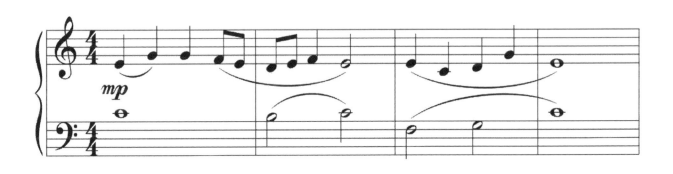

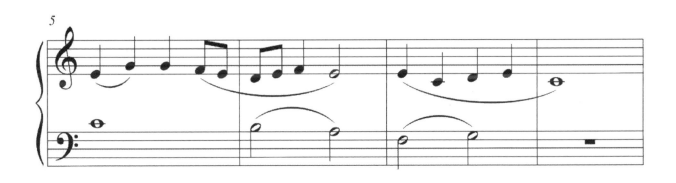

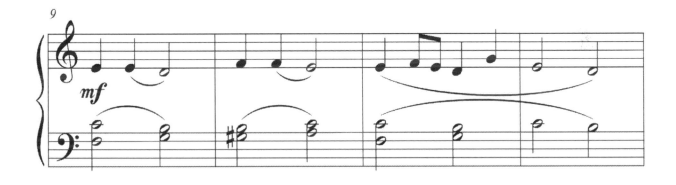

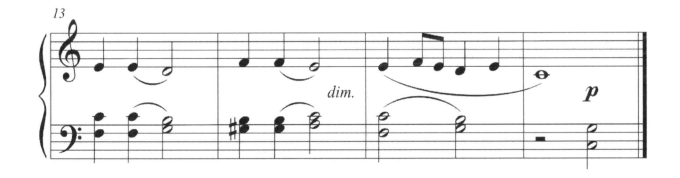

23. A Walk

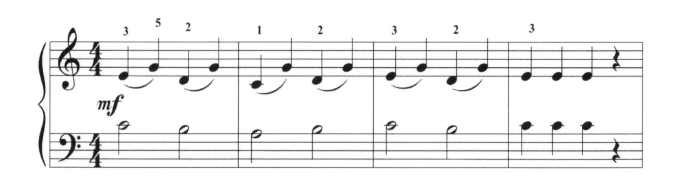

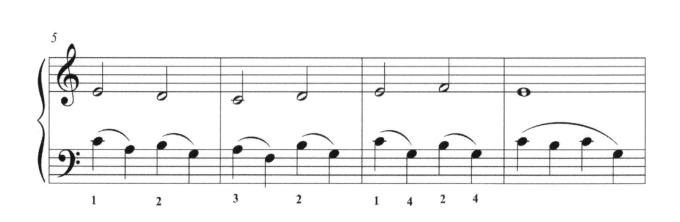

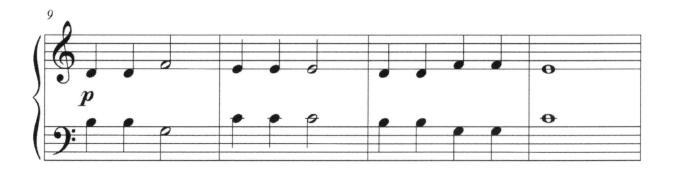

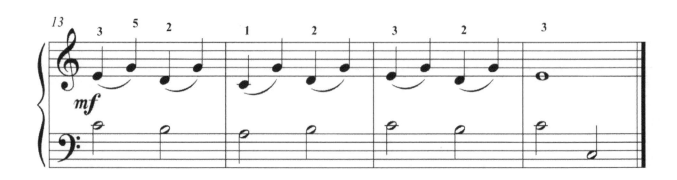

24. Pirate Treasure

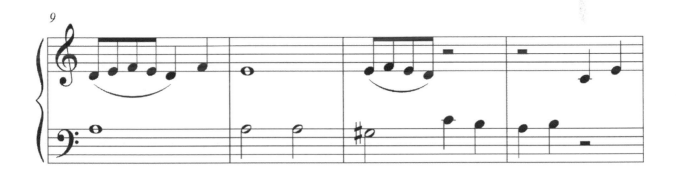

Sorrow

Joanna Bernat

Sunny Day

Joanna Bernat

Printed in Great Britain
by Amazon

45173063R00018